Kentish Town
and Other Loves

Roy Lockett

*For Jeremy
a fine and
entertaining
poet.

Roy*

Hearing Eye

HEARING EYE
TORRIANO MEETING HOUSE
POETRY PAMPHLET SERIES No. 60

Hearing Eye
Box 1, 99 Torriano Avenue
London NW5 2RX, UK
email: books@hearingeye.org
www.hearingeye.org

Acknowledgements
Some poems in this book have appeared in *Morning Star,*
South Bank Poetry, Stage Screen and Radio.

Printed by Catford Print Centre

Cover photographs: Roy Lockett

Design by Martin Parker

Contents

For Dinah
with love and gratitude

Leighton Road

I love the swoop of Leighton Road
glissading down to Kentish Town,
I love her songs, I love her reasons,
her terraced houses and her seasons:
the thirties flats where if you look
you'll find a plaque to Donald Cook
whose rent strike back in sixty-four
shook Camden Council to its core,

the Assembly House where Burton starred,
the gatehouse to our boulevard
where suddenly the sky grows vast
and Hampstead Heath is clear at last
across the railway and the lights,
blue air by day and starred by night,
where on a white hospital roof
that strange menorah stands aloof.

And canopied by London planes
flickered by sun and shone by rains,
the softly cambered speedbumped road
where cyclists mock the highway code
and Russians, Irish and Somalis
engage in endless smiling parleys
and smokers grouped outside the Gloucester
sup Guinness on their endless roster.

Down by the flats in early spring
I've heard the speckled thrushes sing,
seen cherry trees agog with flower
kaleidoscope an April shower,

a spilling sloshing eyeshine gladness
springtime Leighton full of madness
when all the folk of Canteloupe
eat tropic fruit and loop the loop.

We have a secret worth the keeping:
that under us the fields lie sleeping
and country names now label blocks
of flats with beds of hollyhocks,
passed by chattering under-nines
all holding hands in straggly lines:
a new and eager generation
remakes our old north London nation.

The Lost Birds of Kentish Town

Cats enter unoccupied spaces, variety
bleeds away, slides from reality to memory.
The astonishments of shot-silk starlings
with beaks of solid yellow sunlight are edited
from the roughcut of the garden.

Dawn is depleted, only the muttering of early traffic
acknowledges the sullen and unchorused day,
the irreversible hearing loss of a city.
Somewhere an old blackbird in a railway arch
does the honours with solitary élan.

Movement, the flickering periphery, is lost
from pathsides, ruined sheds, paint peeling eaves.
A quick and black-bibbed energy,
the sparrowed world jinking on its axis,
replaced by the stillness of decaying nests.

A black vortex of starlings over London planes
no longer thickens an urban sky at dusk, conspiracies
of sparrows keeping no secrets are gone.
We live with unexpected silences and a kind of emptiness.
More than birds have been lost from Kentish Town.

Brecknock Road

On either side the villas rise,
the rich Victorians' London prize,
the country green of Kentish Town
fresh air to ease their brandy down.
With servants, butlers, maids and more
recruited from the rural poor,
the Breck gave status and good health
to underpin stockbroker wealth.
Today they house a rainbow nation
in laughing, jostling integration.

The Brecknock's side streets tell dark tales
some end with hemp, some end in jails.
Crippen believed strychnine would lead
to rumpled beds with Miss Le Neve;
but as they fled his murdered wife,
sailed for New York and their new life,
Old Bill, still shrewd, had the last laugh,
caught them at sea by telegraph.
Who would guess such seeds were sowed
in quiet treelined Hilldrop Road.

But oh the shops, the tropic fruits,
cumin and herbs, organic roots,
lentils, peas and vegan cheese
for customers at Bumble Bee's.
Our latin love's Salvino's deli,

good parma ham and fine spaghetti,
tomatoes, sweet Sicilian kisses,
mozarella, bread and fishes,
and football argued noon and night,
Spurs'soaring hopes and Arsenal's plight.

The Sunshine fries from eight to five,
ensures our hoodie clans survive,
and satisfies voracious teens
with bacon, chips and eggs and beans
while posties, plumbers, men with cabs,
queue for pizzas and kebabs,
for fish and chips, good veggy soup;
or late at night I've heard them whoop
for roghan josh to take away
and tiger beer to end their day.

The Brecknock marks an ancient border
twixt Islington and its disorder
and Kentish Town's urban delights,
its sundrenched days and throbbing nights,
its Greeks, Italians and Bengalis
now spiced with Russians and Somalis,
new singers of our Brecknock song
who add their verses sweet and strong.
This choir has dreams, knew where to start,
came to the Breck and touched its heart.

Saturday London

I emerge at St Paul's and white light is bouncing off the Cathedral,
a low slung sun, dazzling between Tate Modern's chimneys,
burnishes the heads and shoulders of the crowd walking that sweetly
waisted perforated footbridge over the water into the red brick future.
Everything is full of ease and a man selling the smallest kites in the world
grins at the moth wings flickering on filament, looping,
       tickling the blue strips of Thames and sky, everything is
       brighter than beautiful, Saturday London light and laughing.

Christ it's good here and now, stepping out across the water,
rolling and strolling, knowing everything and anything is possible
and what I want and why I want it, everybody slow and considerate.
Glad I passed up that Circus without Animals in Paradise Street.
Keep thinking of a man in an empty cage with a whip and a chair,
but I'm on the Paradise Bridge in soft slow motion
       with a white sun blazing in my eyes and gulls screaming
       and over the water a brick box spilling wonders waiting.

Then the Turbine Hall, down the longest launching ramp in art history
into the furore of October 1917. Comrades Rodchenko, Meyerhold
and Popova designing factory textiles, building cubist paper sellers' stalls,
demanding the death of easel painting, celebrating the future
in red and black typography. I go into the replica of Rodchenko's
Workers Club, pick up a book of Mayakovsky's poetry. Still reading
       an hour later, thinking about his 'full stop with a bullet' suicide and
       revolutionary art shouldered aside by Stalin's realism.

Then I'm back on the bridge and the sun is softer and the Thames is flatter,
the children are still laughing, everyone is taking digital pictures
but the man with smallest kites in the world has gone.

London Bird Report

Observed and noted in the Bird Report for London
A Great Grey Butcherbird at Kew
A Whitebacked Vulture flying over Croydon
Huge Red Kites scarce but increasing

A great Grey Butcher bird at Kew
A Robin from Wisconsin in a Peckham garden
Huge Red Kites scarce but increasing and
a Nightingale that sang in Wormwood Scrubs

A Robin from Wisconsin in a Peckham Garden
Oystercatchers feeding all along the Thames
A Nightingale that sang in Wormwood Scrubs
Sporting a bell, an Eagle Owl at Thornton Heath

Oystercatchers feeding all along the Thames
an adult Spoonbill seen in Walthamstow
Sporting a bell, an Eagle Owl at Thornton Heath
and drumming Snipe elusive but widespread

An adult Spoonbill seen in Walthamstow
A Whitebacked Vulture flying over Croydon
and drumming Snipe elusive but widespread
Observed and noted in the Bird Report for London

The London Natural History Society publishes the annual London Bird Report based on its members' observations.

Apprenticeship

I left the brickbashers behind me
My Secondary Technical needs
Old Quirky with welding and bossing
Tom Gibson like Lenin in tweeds

Adieu to the 654 trolley
Fizzing up South Norwood hill
Electrical sparks flying freely
Lady Edrich girls out for a thrill

Farewell to the tuppenny Master
Daringly smoked in the park
Goodbye to old Chapman's study,
Canings and making my mark

Leaving tough Rixy from Old Town
And Lacey as sweet as a nut
And Cooper a giant at football
The door to my childhood slammed shut

To Hayward's the old Croydon printers
Where Aunt Doll had got me a job
Fifteen years old and apprenticed
To Patrick, to Dick and to Bob

To droopy old Reynolds the manager
To Gordon just back from the War
The FOC bald Ernie Algar
Enforcing the LSC's law

And ex-Major Marsh the Director
As pissed as a newt in a sack
Passing round Woodbines at Christmas
Hurt that the lads gave them back

Learning the tools and the language
The galleys, the stones and the sticks
The leading, the quoins and the reglets,
Bent chases that no-one could fix

Dissing pied type back in cases
Pulling good proofs on the press
Invoices for Hall and Co depots
All at Marlpit Lane more or less

Victorian woodtype for posters
As pitted and worn as old brick
Driving machine-minders barmy
Makeready half an inch thick

Some jobs were kept standing forever
But charged as if set new each time
Letterheads old as the century
When Hayward was still in his prime

Old curling scripts and worn logos
Arcane as the crown on the press
And that wily old thief Joshua Reynolds
Telling clients he'd set them afresh

Most comps had a rich sense of humour
On the church magazine set by me
Someone changed paddling to piddling
On the pic of the Rev in the sea

Time sheets were works of pure fiction
The timings consistent but odd
The simple jobs overcharged slightly
To make up for the one that's a sod

Apprentices made tea in the mornings
Went out to fat Billy's for rolls
Posted comps' pools on a Friday
At lunchtime took leisurely strolls

To the Temperance Hall to play snooker
Tubby White was the star in those days
The rules were no beer and no whistling
And never smoke over the baize

Tubby could play like Joe Davis
But sometimes he'd miss just for fun
Let you push your score up to forty
Then clear all the balls off in one

The old comps went round to the Greyhound
Among them Dick Goodyer and Pat
Getting stuck into the Guinness
Laughing and chewing the fat

Pat taught me a lot about Ireland
Enniskillen-bred with a Catholic God
Said the old RUC were black bastards
And every last one was a prod

Goodyer was sly and malicious
With an ugly sarcastic wit
He'd whisper our secrets to the Major
Drop all of us lads in the shit

The foreman John Gordon the soldier
In Burma for most of the War
Laughter and song, independent and strong
and hard for the girls to ignore

I learned about trust and betrayal
About pride in your work and your mates
About dignity standing together
About 'Never work under the rates'

Compositors have always been special
Organised, literate, proud
Men who would fight for a principle
Men who stood out in a crowd

One day a week at the College
An old Georgian house by the Hill
High windows and light, extra classes at night
And that learning enriches me still

Private presses, the Bauhaus, Bodoni,
Old Colkett so serious and solemn
Half uncials, Manutius and Morris
Plantin and Trajan's great column

The vast sprawling history of printing,
Technology, graphic design,
Paper weights, colour and half tones
Six years made all of that mine

I went on to Ruskin and Oxford
Worked at the tools in the vac
Hard skills that would never desert me
A life without fear of the sack

Six years is a lifetime at fifteen
And app's pay was a joke even then
But they made me a journeyman printer
And a man and I'd do it again

FOC: Father of the Chapel: Shop Steward in the printers' union.
LSC: London Society of Compositors: Printers' union in 1950s.

Charlie Keen

Charlie was my Dad's oldest friend,
perhaps he was his only friend.
I want to chip his name
into that old red wall of poetry
that winds around and through
the mazy histories of everything
that ever was and how it felt.

He had the character of those old tools
he carried in a grease-stained canvas bag,
strong like the long ropes of wooden beads
he used to bend lead pipes, balanced
and functional as a round-headed mallet,
simple as a lead-tipped bossing stick.
A tough and square-slabbed man
beaten into meaning and value by
the shaping tools of working life
and laughter on London building sites,
an ear-wide grin, a slow and grating voice,
harsh as the pumice of old bricks.
Much tickled by absurdity, his humour
ran like solder on the iron.
A wry and watchful union man,
he laughed at dad's new fifties toryism
which drew soft chuckles from his chest,
and deeply disliked the middle class
who viewed their knocking pipes
like ill-behaved domestic servants
and plumbers as a necessary evil.

He never married until, to general surprise,
my mum matchmade, inviting Mary
on the day that Charlie visited.

After a night of quiet conversation
he asked with deep and formal courtesy
if he could see her home; they left together,
my father stunned, my mother smug.
And in the summer they were married,
my dad still stunned, my mother crying.

But with the virulence of chance,
four summers later his dear Mary died
and left poor Charlie to his trade
and red-eyed memories of comfort's bliss.
He came to see us less.

I saw him last on that November day
when Dad was taken to the crematorium.
Among the flowers laid out on the lawn
was Charlie's bunch of red carnations
with *Happy Landings* written on the card.

Love and Dying

My Mum and Dad were figures
in a landscape of rooms
and scheduled practicality,
inhabitants of other planets
of chemical piping and municipal
administration, lacking passion,
unexpectedness and urgency.
The silken knot of intimacy
no longer laced them.
There were no embraces,
no touching of lips wrapped
in quiet smiles, no funny
special phrases, no secret verses
of body poetry. No shooting stars
that I could ever see.

The great unclenching came
with the power of revelation.
My father's brain convulsed
with a sudden damming of the blood's
red brain routes and his body
lurched into strange immobilities.
Speech clogged, legs recalcitrant,
an arm locked in a shallow V,
thought and action attenuated.

But something utterly new,
startling as morning snow:
gentleness, a smile so filled with love
that it spilled from his face, touching
my mother's arm, her hand, her back,

and such a tenderness in touching
that the chairs and tables danced
for my mother reborn into her beauty,
the sky filled with shooting stars.

My father's huge imperative
could not be deferred:
to reveal the continent of love,
the geology of his life, unmapped
until his wounded brain charted an atlas.
Such a house it was. Full of tears
and delight and the whispering
of beautiful secrets, the silken slipknot
gentling them together.
I remember him moving so slowly,
his good arm reaching, his old eyes
stroking my mother's face, dazzled.

As always, the doctors meant well.
The rationale lucid, the prognosis
rich with promise of revival and new life,
evangelism quick as a surgeon's scalpel.
But healing morphed into survival;
the cuts on Dad's neck
threw his weary brain into stasis.

His eyes were still open,
a gracenote smile hid in his face.
Perhaps he heard words and the engines
of eternity murmuring their power,
perhaps he was as deaf as a stone
between those crisp white sheets.

My mother seated by his bed:
I see her clearly,
her hands budded around my father's,
talking softly to him, hour on hour
about the world of possibilities
for them when he was well,
news bulletins on the garden,
the television programmes she had seen,
tales of their grandchildren.

She sat there while a summer died,
her hands and voice a conduit
of love, a power so enormous that
it ought to have rebuilt a ruined brain,
recharged his limbs, renewed his life,
that sweet repository of all she cared for:
this man lying in Rose Hill Hospital,
the bed awash with sunlight.

The Parish Church

They have used the gravestones to pave
the grassy parklet which replaced
the churchyard, pages from a stone book,
laid neatly end to end. Only the yews
and old stone gate keep faith
with these Croydon dead.

When we were children we believed
that we should be a city,
the Parish Church our Cathedral.
We did not know that old St John's
had once stood second only
to Canterbury, that Whitgift's Palace
of leaded glass and soft red flettons
still stood behind its flying buttresses
and mighty tower, an old hegemony
of Canterbury over our chalk hills,
our mill-rich Wandle shining to the Thames,
a saffron valley on the Archbishop's
road to Portslade and the pebbled sea.
We never knew that six archbishops,
interred in that great chancel, saw
its anthemed perpendicular
as a last step in their ascent to Paradise.

St John's remained a keystone in the arch
of ordinary Croydon lives, a site of grief
for widows of a thousand local men
ruined in the mud and wire of Flanders,
recruited for a shilling by a smiling sergeant

one bright Saturday outside *The Volunteer*
and marched to Mitcham barracks
and an early death. They were mourned
fiercely in that high nave lined with flags
of long-forgotten regiments, the pain
extant and terrible, beating against
the flinted walls.

Butted against that grief, the laughter
of a thousand weddings, the pride,
the Sunday suits, the homburg hats,
the swirly dresses and seven seas of flowers,
the families from Old Town, Pitlake
and the Mitcham Road, riding in big black cars
to walk with due solemnity and secret smiles
though the clustered chatter of neighbours
into the sun-lanced twilight
of the Parish Church, and all the hymns
and prayers and promises wrapped
in the resonance of that great organ,
before the dancing and the drinking and the loving.
On every mantelpiece a photograph
of a confettied couple and the great West Door.

Seen from the high ridge of North End,
the blue grey tower still juts from
the river valley of Old Town, punching
its tiered strength into a Surrey sky.

Smiths Falls

A Canadian uncle rifling my mother's jewelbox:
an old gold brooch, an opal ring, trinkets,
before his furtive airport departure
and my rage red phone call to Canada.
Memory is an old brick falling through water,
each face replaying slow motion film
of his emigration spilling into transportation,
a poster life of prairies and great lakes
offered to a boy grown in London poverty.
The brick turning slowly end over end.

A reality of rotting shingles peeling
from walls, poverty in clean snow:
his fourteen children nurtured by the cold
Canadian cataracts of Smiths Falls.
Thoughts of his dead father across an ocean,
his wealth inherited and unshared.
Fraternal envy of my father, abcessing
into hatred: burnt saplings poking
through deep snow in the fields beside
the Canadian Pacific line to Ottawa.

Fifty years later I'm in winter Canada,
astonished by scale and snow and sky,
visiting my partner's cousin in Kingston
on the Smiths Falls line.
The old fury writhes back into life.
I remember my mother crying, my father
bruised by something close to grief,
robbed by a brother because of an
imagined inheritance from a father
who gave nothing away, alive or dead.

Siren keening dark and sudden arias,
the high train drills a tapering tunnel
through the vast black Canadian night,
the window leached of expectations.
Somewhere in the vortex of family history
and the invisible snowfields lapping the tracks
is Smiths Falls and the edge of madness.
The train is hot and tidy, the passengers
talk quietly as though they anticipate
a minor event entailing mythology and pain.

We halt at Fallowfield, a glimpse of road,
two streetlights and a picket fence. We move on,
thirty minutes of darkness without shape
and a soft voice announces
Les Cataracts de Smith, Smiths Falls.
The town is taken hostage by the night.
Smiths Falls is a single lighted Hopper window,
separate and unanchored to the world.
A rectangle of booking hall,
a grey-haired man mops with slow strokes.

The corroded timebomb, fifty years of anger
is defused by this invisibility,
this astonishing absence of identity.
The man with the mop moves slowly across the window.
I return to my seat, the panic subsides.
The train lurches, the window slides out of my life.
Impassive darkness returns.
Smiths Falls hides its face in black Ontario snow.
One side of a brick,
falling slowly, end over end.

Blackthorn

has the impatience of young love,
eager to be about its business.
Unlike the ordered hawthorn
moving in a grown-up way
from April greening leaf
to May's massed flower,
Blackthorn cannot wait,
ejaculates its snow-burst blossom
before it can be dealing
with the duller work
of making leaves
and sharpening young thorns.
Hundreds of yards of hedgerow
reborn from winter sticks
to scented barricades,
chrome white dabbed and streaked
across the landscape,
offering everything,
here and now, today.

Bugger the leaves.

Melding Seasons

The curve of the seasons
is softening on the axes
of temperature and time.
Points on the curve record
fat green aphids,
December daffodils,
winter bees bewildered
by untimely light.

Temper is leaching
from the temperature,
frost is frailer and less of it,
the wind's roar discards
its cold ache, the deep
clay shrinks and cracks
to a slow schedule.
The exoskeletons of old
houses twist and fracture,
the certainties of earth
are steadily denied.
Fierce rowan roots
pierce and pursue
the quiet retraction
of the water.

The curve flattens further
across the graph
of the landscape,
a watercolour wash
of pale ochre
stains the paper.

The Burying Way

Today we walk the Burying Way,
the wide grassed track across the fields
beside loosestrifed ditches hogweed high
under a white-gold sun in an
enormous blue Cambridgeshire sky,
a quiet landscape strolling into summer.

Ten miles away the timber tower of Ely
juts above a smudge of woodland
in this reformed and roundhead landscape
of drained fens and black earth
fields as wide as history and rich
as Dutch engineers could make them.

This old green road led solemn village mourners
from Little Thetford to Stretham church
where proper rites could be observed
before the coffined cart returned
to Thetford graveyard, grown from lichened stone,
dressed with oxslips and cowparsley.

Today our dog dives into weedy ditches:
splutters, shakes, sequined with duckweed.
For Labradors water is a kind of madness
and it is a day for anarchic dogs.
We pause, smiling at each other
in the grey gold shadows of old ash trees.

The pea fields flow into the horizon,
silver green leaves and thick fat pods entangled
by curly fusewire tendrils clambering up into
that bright Anglian light. We fill a hat
with peas, a benison of the Burying Way,
where Stretham steeple beckons the dead.

Collective Nouns

Always a piteousness of doves
loose and lovely as bee drifts
over a skulk of foxes and
hard trading by a business of ferrets

Loose and lovely as bee drifts
a dissimulation of small birds
hard trading by a business of ferrets,
tidings of magpies shouting at God

A dissimulation of small birds
over a skulk of foxes and
tidings of magpies shouting at God
above an assiduous labour of moles

Over a skulk of foxes and
a white wedge of swans,
above an assiduous labour of moles
a richesse of skimming martins

A white wedge of swans
over a skulk of foxes and
a richesse of skimming martins
Always a piteousness of doves

English Fantasy

The train is arriving at Bicester North
from which I and my darling will some day set forth
for the lost towns of England and the villages hidden
in the green of the hills and the roads that are ridden
only by cyclists with windscattered hair
and the joy of their wheels and the sky's tinny glare.

To the obstinate oak now encircled by wheat
and the hawthorny hedge and the sedge leafy sweet
in faded March grass and the slow stream's green dreams
where the land is as true and as old as it seems.
In the tussocky fields, the striped swell of the hill
where ploughshares have carded the earth like a mill

and the conkery gleam in the eyes of the beasts
suggests best Sunday china, and roasting and feasts
while skylarks are spiralling the staircase of sky
to a blue air of music in the shine of God's eye
and churches are kneeling beneath prayerful clouds
where pulpits and chancels and roodscreens are bowed

and stones in the graveyards, assembled and still,
stand in handfolded reverence, submit to His will.
There yew trees are pious and small birds audacious
and celandine, bluebell and oxslip are gracious,
and farmland and heathland and downland delight
in the bright of the morning and star silvered night.

Oh one day my darling we will sally forth
on an old and a slow road from Bicester North.

Fellside Church

From Brigsteer the road climbs steeply
to a sky which arcs for fifty miles across
the ragged hills to Morecambe and a pewter sea.
We cross the fell face to a gritstone wall,
a long grey scarf knotted loosely round
the garlic flowered graveyard, enclosing
the tilted stones of Kendal Anglicans,
loyally laid in sad families of grieving mothers,
upright fathers and dead children.

Green and yellow lichens ease across
the names and dates, soften the stone
price tags of old and terrible winters
in this high place of wind and cold and grace,
paint the rootstones of the tiny hunkered church,
walls pierced by clear glass lancets. Stripes
of fell light hatch colour in the yellow oak
of pews and pulpit dedicated to dead deacons,
freshen the white silk lilies and pink roses
of altarcloths embroidered by tired women
working by lamplight after long days
carding wool, cooking, waiting to warm beds.

At the west end, behind a drooping purple rope,
there is a desk with broken hymnals, envelopes,
blunt pencils and a pile of fading postcards.
A church too small for a vestry, resigned
to parson's disregard for tidiness because
it is a practical place, providing solace
for shepherds who learned long ago
that prayer and self-reliance dovetail sweetly,
have small use for gilded angels in a vaulted nave.

Gaza

A poem does not kill:
but what has poetry to offer
the burned and dying
the bulldozed homes
the broken orchards and the roofless byres?

Poetry will not stitch a wound
deliver sacks of flour
decontaminate a well
make bricks or sharpen tools,
extinguish white phosphorus
burning on a child's face,
fend off flechettes
cartwheeling in soft bodies.

No poem is able to record
the decibels of human grief,
or images of shellbursts
at twenty eight frames per second.

A poem is everything it cannot do
measured against
                      a scatter of words.

Iceland

A dozen miles away a fan of blue and violet light
spills from a torn pearled sky staining a snowfield
and the glacier-rounded mountain at its heart.
Iceland has opened a vein, bleeds into the dusk

above that furrow ploughed by an old god,
a deep black trench, sheer-sided, slabbed and winding
through a broken snow-heaped landscape
where children play between the jaws of continents

and watchful parents, eyes edged with ancient fear,
give human scale to this great ice-scabbed wound
where Europe and America collide and magma slides,
locked in a tectonic agony of birth and death.

Iceland does not hide earth's red and liquid strength.
Boiling steam explodes from porous rock.
Islands burn like scarlet lanterns in the blue silk night.
Cloudy with pumice, hot water seethes and rises.

In this theatre of flame and snow and marvels,
an idea grew, like a midnight sun illuminating
the minds and lives of Viking colonists, finding
its locus in that long rifted world-dividing valley

where men from every compass point unearthed
a common lodestone and identity in difference,
a glorious rediscovery of democracy amid
low mountains drawn in snow and charcoal,

and made an Althing, parliament for all the people,
declared a new Icelandic commonwealth,
recast the old alloy of feudalism, became
a land of virtuous pagans speaking freely.

Today Icelanders shout for promises unkept
in a mirage of avarice and glittering citied steel,
a righteous anger freighted with history
sees through the steam a house of cards.

People gathering in the streets,
the Althing's windows crazed by stones,
a new history is being written,
the sky still leaking violet light.

Pembrokeshire Snow

In the quietness which fills the yard
in the absence of the children,
I finish scraping ice off the Ford,
walk to the open gate and turn
into a narrow sloping lane
between ramparts of broken bracken
and yellow flecked gorse, clumpy
with platforms of snow,
all backlit by a blue ice sky,
empty and cold as a small eternity,
blending me with the silence
of the forgiving snow,
offering renewal,
recording every step I take.

Dinah

You bless me with the softness of the kiss
   and with your trust so fragile and entire
Your smile a duning of the heart's wonder
Your hand's touch a question and a resolution
Your quietness in sleep a budded lily
Your waking a slow turning to the sun
Your mornings and your evenings
   the ends of rainbows and the edge of stars
Your life a Turner painting of a sky
   that stuns my eye and stills my heart
So luminous, so luminous my love

Helsington and Moira

I remember you walking slowly, hunched
against the wind, back across the fell
between the trees, high branches arching
over a small figure cocooned in memories,
the only movement under a white sky
scaled with pearl and silver, heading
towards the small wreath of yellow flowers
resting against that old white stone.
Your father sits in a folding chair,
wrapped in a green tartan rug, staring
across the valley at the broken nosed headland
butting into the sky, a bruiser's profile
scenting the salt-edged wind
from Morecambe and a flat steel sea.

We have come every year since your mother died
and we sowed her ashes on the fellside
up here in Helsington where birdsong
is muted by soft grey light and a small church
nests in a stone walled graveyard.
We are remembering the grain of Moira's face
and the colours of her laughter,
recalling that old sepia photograph,
a Kendal schoolgirl in gossamer with fairy wings,
waiting for the magic to begin.

Lyric

Oh I will wrap you in soft sheets of poetry
Hum tunes so sweet your eyes will turn to sky
Plant seven seas of flowers at your doorstep
And never ask you when or where or why

I'll sail you to the furthest edge of wonder
Watch triremes gliding by with golden sails
Fly with a swoop of swallows into sunsets
Amuse you with a thousand thrilling tales

Entertain you with a magic concertina
Pleated with stars that glitter at your noon
Watch you dance flamenco with an angel
And make you laugh beneath a grinning moon

Brush your red, red hair with musky roses
Shine gentle honeyed light into your room
Weave tiny threads of love into your bodice
Sweep all your floors up with a jinking broom

I will learn to sew and knit bright dresses
Cut rolls of sky and smiling suns aright
Stitch neatly all the coloured squares of love
Into a soaring silken patchwork kite

We'll fly our kite high over happy Hampstead
Northumbria, the Lakes and Brighton beach
And crowds will stand and watch in great amazement
At just how far two people's love can reach

Rondeau for Jack Amos

I sing Joe Hill, of means and ends,
with communists, his kin and friends,
who mark Jack's death in Kentish Town
when snow made streets as soft as down,
and now the grief and music blends

at Golders Green; a banner bends
in stained glass light its silk descends.
For him and his hard earned renown
I sing Joe Hill.

There are no prayers, no hymn offends
the measured grace that reason lends
this man who waved and did not drown
made Union Jack his laughing noun.
For all that brotherhood defends,
the values that his life commends,
We sing Joe Hill.